PRAYER:
A SPIRITUAL WEAPON OF
MASS DESTRUCTION

Volume 1

Praying the
Books of Ephesians,
Colossians, Philemon, and
Philippians

VALERIE MECCA

Table of Contents

Use This Book

This book can be used as a tool for daily prayer time to pray God's Will to be done on Earth as it is in heaven. According to Matthew 6:10, *"your kingdom come, your will be done, on earth as it is in heaven."* It is important to memorize and meditate on scriptures found in this book and the Bible.

Fill yourself with the Word of God, become a doer of the Word, hide the Word in your heart that you might not sin against the Lord. Live the fruitful holy life God wants you to live. According to Psalm 119:11, *"I have hidden your word in my heart that I might not sin against you."*

Become a radically transformed Christian where the love of God is shed abroad in your heart by the Holy Spirit. Be an example of God's love so that those around you would choose to have a close, intimate relationship with Christ Jesus.

My suggestion is to include daily Bible reading, Bible study, praise, worship, singing in the spirit and praying in the spirit to grow closer to the Lord. Allow Him to saturate you with His Perfect Love which casts out all fear.

It will bring peace, joy, breakthrough, blessings and so much more. According to 1 John 4:18 (NKJV), *"There is no fear in love; but perfect love casts out fear, because fear involves torment. But he who fears has not been made perfect in love."*

It is important to speak the scriptures out loud. After all, Father God spoke creation into existence by the Prophetic Word. He called those things that are not as though they were. According to Romans 4:17 (NKJV), God *"calls those things which do not exist as though they did."*

The Bible teaches us how to live our lives according to God's way, not as the world would have us live. We are to conform to God's standards, which are righteousness and holiness.

About This Book

This book was titled "PRAYER: A SPIRITUAL WEAPON OF MASS DESTRUCTION, Volume 1, Praying the Books of Ephesians, Colossians, Philemon, and Philippians," because God's Word does not return void and will accomplish what it was sent to do. According to Isaiah 55:11 (NKJV), "*So shall My word be that goes forth from My mouth; It shall not return to Me void, But it shall accomplish what I please, And it shall prosper in the thing for which I sent it.*"

It separates the soul from the spirit, provides breakthrough, deliverance, and brings forth life. According to Hebrews 4:12, "*For the word of God is alive and active. Sharper than any double-edged sword, it penetrates even to dividing soul and spirit, joints and marrow; it judges the thoughts and attitudes of the heart.*"

It sets the captives free in the Name of Jesus. It moves mountains, raises valleys and makes the crooked places straight. According to Isaiah 45:2 (NKJV), "*I will go before you And make the crooked places straight; I will break in pieces the gates of bronze And cut the bars of iron.*"

It is a powerful weapon that when used, will accomplish that which it was intended to do. According to 2 Corinthians 10:4 (NASB), "*for the weapons of our warfare are not of the flesh, but divinely powerful for the destruction of fortresses.*"

Start with Faith Scriptures

Mark 11:24, *"Therefore I tell you, whatever you ask for in prayer, believe that you have received it, and it will be yours."*

James 5:16 (NKJV), *"Confess your trespasses to one another, and pray for one another, that you may be healed. The effective, fervent prayer of a righteous man avails much."*

Hebrews 11:6, *"And without faith it is impossible to please God, because anyone who comes to him must believe that he exists and that he rewards those who earnestly seek him."*

Dedication

To Father God who has a great plan for our lives. According to Jeremiah 29:11 (NKJV), "*For I know the thoughts that I think toward you, says the* LORD, *thoughts of peace and not of evil, to give you a future and a hope.*"

Thank You, Lord, for loving us (me, my husband Paul, our daughter Arianna, our son Paul, our child that was miscarried in 1992, our future daughter-in-law, our future son-in-law, our families, all of our bloodline, all our future descendants, all those we love, our Brothers and Sisters in Christ, leaders in the United States of America, leaders across the globe, and all mankind).

Thank You for saving us, setting us free and allowing us to have eternity in heaven with You. Lord help us to seek You with all of our hearts, and find You. According to Deuteronomy 4:29, "*But if from there you seek the* LORD *your God, you will find him if you seek him with all your heart and with all your soul.*" Lord, continue to reveal the plans You have for each of our lives; help us to be obedient to You.

Help us to confess and repent of our sins daily and to follow You regardless of the cost. According to James 5:16, "*Therefore confess your sins to each other and pray for each other so that you may be healed. The prayer of a righteous person is powerful and effective.*"

Thank You, Father God, for loving us so very much and giving us Your Only Begotten Son who shed His precious sinless Blood for us.

According to John 3:16, *"For God so loved the world that he gave his one and only Son, that whoever believes in him shall not perish but have eternal life."*

Thank You for helping us to overcome by the Blood of the Lamb and the Word of our Testimony which brings deliverance to others. According to Revelation 12:11, *"They triumphed over him by the blood of the Lamb and by the word of their testimony."*

To Christ Jesus, Our Savior, thank You for coming down from heaven, walking the Earth as a mere man, taking our sins to the cross, being crucified, dying a horrific death and miraculously rising from the dead. You overcame death and forever live to make intercession for each and every one of us while seated at the right hand of the Father God.

According to Romans 8:34 (NKJV), *"It is Christ who died, and furthermore is also risen, who is even at the right hand of God, who also makes intercession for us."* Thank You for all you continuously do for us.

To the Holy Spirit, our Spiritual GPS, thank You for guiding and leading us in the way we should go. According to Psalm 32:8 (NKJV), *"I will instruct you and teach you in the way you should go; I will guide you with My eye."* You are always with us and will never forsake us. According to John 14:26 (NKJV), *"But the Helper, the Holy Spirit, whom the Father will send in My name, He will teach you all things, and bring to your remembrance all things that I said to you."*

Thank You for comforting us and convicting us when the words that we speak and the meditation of our hearts are not pleasing to You. Thank You for being an inner witness to us, confirming what You want us to do, where You want us to go, what You want us to speak, and what You want us to meditate on in all things.

Help us to be mindful of what we allow to go into our eye and ear gate, and most importantly what comes out of our mouths, because out of the abundance of our hearts, our mouths speak. According to Luke 6:45 (NKJV), *"For out of the abundance of the heart the mouth speaks."*

Lord, help us to hide Your Word in our hearts that we do not sin against You. According to Psalm 119:11, *"I have hidden your word in my heart that I might not sin against you."*

To my loving husband, best friend, confidant and my cheerleader, Paul, who I love with all my heart. Your support throughout my life is priceless. Thank you for encouraging me to be my best self. I thank God for you!

To my adult children Arianna and Paul, who I love with all my heart. Thank you for inspiring and encouraging me and for the joy you bring into my life. I thank God for both of you!

To my parents and grandmother, who showed love and support throughout my life and encouraged me to move forward, overcoming the opposition. To my siblings, for the good times, love and support I have experienced. To all of my family and in-laws, I love you very much.

To Apostle Judi Valencia, Pat Cavallo, and Church of God (COG) State Intercessor Garzarella, who the Lord used to be my spiritual mothers, cheering me on to keep moving forward in the things of God. Your love, prayers, support and friendship are priceless. I love you very much.

For all my Brothers and Sisters in Christ who I met along the way while attending courses, trainings, teachings, and those with whom I co-labored with in

11

ministry on Prayer and Healing teams. I am so blessed to know each of you.

To every person I have met along the way from birth to present, you have played a role in my life. I love you.

Endorsements

"My dear wife Valerie, tireless prayer warrior, who dwells in the Secret Place of the Most High. Her book is to encourage and equip the saints through prayer, both young and seasoned. May her prayers resonate with your Spirit to ignite your prayer life to new levels and perspectives. God bless all those that read Valerie's first of many prayer books, that they would be compelled to share their experience and bless others. Amen."
–Paul Mecca, Valerie's other half and husband of over 30 years

"The author shares her own experience of developing a fruitful prayer life. A helpful guide for beginners seeking inspiration as well as for those already on this journey."
– Marilynn C. Koller – colleague and longtime friend

"Valerie Mecca has a heart to see every believer grounded in God's word. The Book *Prayer: A Spiritual Weapon of Mass Destruction, Volume 1, Praying the Books of Ephesians, Colossians, Philemon, and Philippians*, gives us clear guidance in how we can live our lives according to God's standard and ways. This book will not only give you a greater insight into God's ways but will also help you to develop a deeper understanding as you pray these prayers yourself. The principles in this book will help you develop a biblically-centered prayer life."

– Kim Corden - Founder of "The Light Line." Intercessory services. www.thelightline.net

"Valerie is a woman after God's heart. She loves the Lord, loves people, loves to pray and share her faith with others. Her prayers are from the heart. The Lord joined us together in prayer when we met during a church sponsored training in 2017. We sensed the Holy Spirit had a purpose for us to partner in prayer. To this day, we pray together on a regular basis, intercede, and stand in the gap. We love to pray the Word of God together, the practice of which is demonstrated through this book. My prayer is that the Lord bless and move mightily by His Spirit to bring forth His Will; releasing the power of His Word in each of us, among us in the Body of Christ, and through us mightily for His plans to be fulfilled. His will and plan are for the benefit of all people He has created and truly loves. This book is timely because it is now a vital season for each person to seek the Lord, to pray personally and together in agreement. May we pray, unite, and agree together with the Lord, His Word, and His Kingdom purposes in the Name of Jesus Christ, our Lord and Savior. Lord Jesus be glorified, for You are our Soon and Coming King of kings and Lord of lords!"

– Joann Garzarella - Church of God (COG)
  State Intercessor

"Even as we are told in Scripture that the worlds were prepared by the Word of God, as we pray, declare, and decree His word, it becomes a creative and mighty weapon in our war against the enemy of our souls. Valerie Mecca has compiled a manual of Spirit-breathed prayers and declarations using the Word of God so we can have His power to change the atmosphere of our hearts, our homes, our communities and our nation right at our fingertips. Our God is watching over His word to perform it (Jeremiah 1:12) and we know His angels perform His word, and obey the voice of His word (Psalm 103:20). Let us stand and decree His promises and see His eternal victory established in all that concerns us as believers in His Name!"

– Jane Schoonover, Coordinator of Intercessory Prayer for
* The Breakthrough Prayer Call*

"I've heard it said, 'You've got to pray just to make it today.'" Never have these words been more true than in this time in which we live. We are facing a universal unparalleled invasion of the powers of hell such as we have never seen before. Although prayer is a multifaceted subject, it is clear that it is a most powerful weapon in engaging the spiritual battles going on around us and in us. Valerie Mecca's book about prayer as a weapon of mass destruction most certainly will be of great assistance in destroying the works of the enemy. Join in agreement with these scriptural based prayers and watch the power of the Holy Spirit manifested through the finished work of Jesus Christ."

– Rev. Chris A. Fraley, Senior Pastor, Abundant Life
* Church of God, Freehold, New Jersey, USA*

"A delightful guide, full of important information for those of us who need encouragement in prayer and clear specific direction for prayer growth. This book is wonderfully written and is a good companionship with the Bible in your quiet time of prayer."

– Pastor Patricia Bowden, Breakthrough in Christ
* Ministries*

Preface

A few months after being touched by Holy Spirit, I was led to a teaching and training church. After service one Sunday, I approached the Church Founder and Senior Pastor asking "How do you pray those great prayers? I want to be able to pray like that too." He recommended the "Prayers that Avail Much" book by Germaine Copeland. I read through the book numerous times, practically cover to cover. My appetite for being able to pray and speak scriptures continued to expand as I heard others praying and speaking scriptures in my classes. Even in conversation with some of the students, they would speak scriptures as declarations of faith. According to Hebrews 4:12, *"For the word of God is alive and active. Sharper than any double-edged sword, it penetrates even to dividing soul and spirit, joints and marrow; it judges the thoughts and attitudes of the heart."* Determination started to rise in me.

Although it was a struggle in the beginning, I continued to pray and ask God to help me. I made it a point to intentionally make use of my time and listened to scriptures as I slept trying to fill myself with the Word of God as much as I could.

I enrolled in many foundational courses offered at church to get a good biblical foundation and be free from wrong teachings, worldliness and lies of the enemy. These courses helped me to be connected to church on a regular basis during the week as well as regularly attending Sunday Service. It brought greater exposure to scripture reading and hearing the Word of God. My spirit was being filled with the Word of God and sound biblical teachings which helped to root out the old ways and brought forth new ways of thinking, speaking, and acting. I was being set free from the lies and was being filled with the Truth. According to Galatians 6:7 (NKJV), "*Do not be deceived, God is not mocked; for whatever a man sows, that he will also reap.*"

Although it was frustrating to not make the significant progress right away, over time after pressing in I started to see the results I longed for.

As I continued to exercise this process, asking others to pray for me and having faith in God that He would make it happen, I experienced results suddenly!

One day while reading the Bible, I was able to pray the scriptures. Just like that! Over time, praying scriptures became easier. It was a melody to my heart. I was filled with joy and excitement. The Lord helped me overcome barriers and be successful in praying the scriptures.

What God has done for me, He will do for you because He is no respecter of persons. According to Romans 2:11, "*For God does not show favoritism.*"

This book was created to help you pray the Word of God in a timely and efficient manner that aligns with His Word and Plan.

Another desire of my heart is to help the Body of Christ grow in the power of prayer to bring about God's Will to be done on Earth as it is in heaven.

When our hearts turn to God in prayer and we stand in the gap, having one hand in heaven and one hand on Earth, interceding on behalf of our family, our relatives, the Body of Christ, our neighbors, our communities, our state, our nation, and all people across the globe, we will see miraculous transformation such as divine encounters, the manifestation of God's Presence, strongholds being broken, and deliverance from evil. According to James 5:16 (NKJV), *"The effective, fervent prayer of a righteous man avails much."*

Acknowledgments

Thank you to those who have contributed their time, resources, and talent towards the effort of writing the book.

Editor: Marilynn C. Koller

Photographer of Back Cover Photo:
Paul J. Mecca - jpaul.photo@yahoo.com

Foreword

"I have been in the ministry of the Lord for almost 40 years now, as a Pastor, Bible Teacher, Prayer Leader, Prophet, and Revivalist. I am now in my current position of Head Apostle of an Apostolic Revival and Training Center.

I first came to know Valerie Mecca in one of the Women's Bible Study classes that I was teaching about 12 years ago. During the time that I first met Valerie, I found myself being introduced to a woman who had a genuine hunger to know God in an intimate way and to grow in the knowledge and pursuit of Him. Since that time, I have had the privilege of seeing Valerie blossom into a beautiful, Spirit-filled believer in the Lord Jesus Christ. She truly has a deep love for the Lord, His Church, and for those who do not yet know Him. Valerie has a deep desire to bring others into the fulfilling relationship with Jesus that she herself has come to know.

I remember the first time I met Valerie Mecca. She left an impression on me because of her eagerness, hunger and humility. She had, and still has, a true love for people. Valerie is always willing to take the time to give a word of encouragement to someone that needs one. She is always there with a helping hand and a smile. When I first met Valerie, she had a pure vulnerability and I found her to be very teachable in her pursuit of God. She just wanted to learn and grow in the things of God. She was the perfect student. Her desire to see others learn and grow developed into her inviting every friend and woman she knew to join her in her spiritual journey. Our Bible Study class grew with Valerie's influence. Today, she is ready to teach others the basics of Christianity and prayer that she has learned.

This desire to bring others into the saving knowledge of Jesus and to help them grow, lives stronger than ever in Valerie's heart today. Valerie has allowed her gifts and talents to be used for the Lord. She has the heart of an Intercessor and the heart of an Evangelist. These gifts are seen throughout the pages of this book. Her desire is to teach others the truths she has learned along the way and to help them find the joy and freedom that she has found in Christ.

As you, yourself, apply the Bible truths and principles in this book, you will begin to experience the same joy and freedom that Valerie has found.

The Bible teaches us in the Gospel of John, the words of Jesus to His disciples:

"Then you will know the truth, and the truth will set you free." John 8:32

The Bible is God's word of truth to us. As you read and pray the scriptures from God's word in this book, "Prayer: A Spiritual Weapon of Mass Destruction," you will find a supernatural and spiritual power in your life that will truly set you free. As you pray and meditate on God's word, a transformation will begin to take place in your heart and mind. You will begin to discover a peace and a joy that you hadn't experienced before.

I, also, share in Valerie's desire to see you know and experience God's perfect love for you. It will change your life, heal your heart and enrich your relationships. I encourage you to use this book, along with your Bible, in your prayer and devotional time. It is a tool to assist you on your spiritual journey and will bring enlargement to your prayer life. May God bless you as you open the pages of this book and become "a spiritual weapon" yourself: a person who knows their God and knows how to pray His prayers!"

> – *Rev. Judith Valencia*
> Head Apostle
> Christian Revival Center
> Toms River, New Jersey
> Author of the Book: *"The Emerging Warrior Bride: A Prophetic Revelation of the Bridal Paradigm"*

Book Description

The intention of this book is to assist in a fruitful prayer life, to see prayers avail much, connect with Almighty God in the Name of Jesus and feel the anointing of Holy Spirit. This book was inspired by Almighty God through the Holy Spirit in the Name of Jesus to take the Holy Scriptures from the Book of Ephesians, Colossians, Philemon, and Philippians and use them as a basis for prayer foundation. Praying the Holy Scriptures is praying the Will of God, which is extremely powerful.

- Did you know Almighty God's breath is on each page of the Bible?

- Have you ever wondered how to pray the Holy Scriptures?

- Do you know someone who can pray prayers that touch your heart?

- Do you want to grow in a relationship with Almighty God and pray His Will to be done on Earth as it is in heaven?

If so, this book is for you. Today and in the days ahead, we will need to pray more for ourselves and to intercede on behalf of others.

Prayer moves the Hand of God. We need to have God's blessings, health, healing, wholeness, safety, protection, provision, wisdom, discernment, knowledge, understanding, guidance, direction and all His promises upon our lives, those we love, the Body of Christ, all leaders, local and across the globe.

The decisions (or lack thereof) that leaders make in the Seven Mountains of Society – (Government, Media, Arts and Entertainment, Business, Education, Religion, and Family) affect everyone throughout the whole world, even extending to future generations.

Absence of prayer allows the enemy to gain ground, but our prayers can expand our territory and take back all that has been lost and stolen, giving us back even more in Jesus' name. Shouldn't that be something every believer in Christ would want? Therefore we need to pray for our bloodline, our future descendants, the Body of Christ and leaders throughout the world because in the days ahead, gross darkness will cover the Earth. We need to be holy ambassadors for Christ, doing our part by taking action and praying.

We need to know what the Bible says, what our part is and take action to do what God asks of us.

After all, it should be the desire of every person to want to hear the beautiful words when they meet with Almighty God face-to-face and hear, *"Well done, good and faithful servant!"* (Matthew 25:23). Nothing else will do.

Introduction

The foundation of this book is based on the Books of Ephesians, Colossians, Philemon, and Philippians. Prayer is one of the tools the Lord gives His people, the saints, as a spiritual weapon of mass destruction. It will assist you to pray prayers that avail much, that align with heaven combating the forces of darkness and bringing forth God's Will on Earth as it is in heaven.

According to James 5:16 (NASB), *"Therefore, confess your sins to one another, and pray for one another so that you may be healed. The effective prayer of a righteous man can accomplish much."*

As you learn and grow in the things of God, use your gifts and talents to help others grow in their gifts and talents.

We, as the Body of Christ, need to edify each other, locking arms together as an army of the Lord to see His Will be done on Earth as it is in heaven. After all, we are family in the spirit realm.

Paraphrased from Willmington's Guide to the Bible (page 467):

The Book of Ephesians – presents Christ is the head of the invisible church.

The Book of Colossians – presents Christ is the head of the Church where the emphasis is on Christ.

The Book of Philemon – presents Christians living in a pagan society.

The Book of Philippians – presents Christian living with Christ - I can do all things through Christ who gives me strength (Philippians 4:13).

Salvation and Eternal Life

To be saved and have eternal life is vital. Eternity is forever, not like life on Earth which is temporal.

Each heart has a void that only The Lord, Christ Jesus can fill. There is only One True satisfaction and that can only be found in Jesus. According to Romans 10:13, *"Everyone who calls on the name of the Lord will be saved."*

If you have not already confessed and repented of your sins, ask Jesus to forgive you and invite Him into your heart to be your Lord and Savior. I suggest you pray this prayer before moving forward.

According to James 5:16, *"Therefore confess your sins to each other and pray for each other so that you may be healed. The prayer of a righteous person is powerful and effective."*

Salvation Prayer

Prayer of Salvation -

"Lord Jesus, I believe You are the Son of God. Thank You for dying on the cross for my sins. I repent of my sins. Come into my heart, wash me clean, I'll make You my Lord and Savior. Amen."

Oración de Salvación -

"Señor Jesús, creo que tú eres el Hijo de Dios. Gracias por morir en la cruz por mis pecados. Me arrepiento de mis pecados. Ven a mi corazón, limpiame, Te recibo como mi Señor y Salvador. Amén."

Confession of Sins

According to 1 John 1:9, *"If we confess our sins, He is faithful and just and will forgive us our sins and purify us from all unrighteousness."*

According to James 5:16, *"Therefore confess your sins to each other and pray for each other so that you may be healed. The prayer of a righteous person is powerful and effective."*

It is best to confess our sins, repent of our sins, and ask for Almighty God's forgiveness before praying to Him in the Name of Jesus. It creates in us clean hands and a pure heart (Psalm 24:4) as we approach Our Holy God in His Throne of Grace (Hebrews 4:16).

Prayer to Confess My Sins

Father God, I desire to come to You with clean hands and a pure heart as written in Psalm 24:4, as I approach Your Throne of Grace. Your Word says according to 1 John 1:9, *"If we confess our sins, You are faithful and just to forgive us our sins and cleanse us from all unrighteousness."* Lord thank You for being faithful to Your Word.

According to Numbers 23:19 (NKJV), *"God is not a man, that He should lie, Nor a son of man, that He should repent. Has He said, and will He not do? Or has He spoken, and will He not make it good?"*

Lord, I confess my sins and the sins of all mankind of everything that has not been pleasing in Your sight, including: arrogance, arguing, anger, animosity, jealousy, greed, judging, control, self-centeredness, self-righteousness, criticizing, murmuring, complaining, entitlement, rebellion, selfishness, pride, accusations, fear, panic, worry, stress, anxiety, offense, oppression, depression, not representing You correctly, not inquiring of You throughout our day in our decisions no matter how big or small, not taking every thought captive to the obedience of Christ, not taking good care of our body which is the temple of the Holy Spirit, not exercising enough, not getting enough rest, not eating healthy as we ought, not reverencing You, Lord, the way that You deserve, forsaking the assembly of the brethren, being people pleasers instead of God pleasers, not honoring our mother and father, not being doers of the Word in all areas of our lives, not teaching and training our children in the Lord, having false idols, looking to man instead of You, putting things before You and making

You second best instead of our best, not asking or allowing You to order our footsteps, not guarding our hearts, minds and mouths, allowing things to be exalted above You, trying to fight our battles in our own strength, not being obedient to You, not trusting You, not forgiving as we ought, everything we have done, are doing and will do that is not pleasing in Your sight whether knowingly or unknowingly, every evil work and every kind of sin past, present, and future. We confess and ask for Your Forgiveness, Mercy and Grace.

Repent For My Sins & Pray

It is best to repent for our sins, which will help us to not fall into temptation (Matthew 26:41). It creates in us a humble heart (Psalm 51:10) as we speak to a Holy God who sits on His Throne of Grace (Hebrews 4:16).

PRAYERS TO REPENT OF MY SINS

Father God, I repent with a sincere, remorseful heart, desiring to turn away from my sins. I repent for me, my household (state each name), our family, our ancestors, our bloodline, our future descendants, all of our families, the Body of Christ and all mankind ever created, past, present and future, for everything that was not pleasing in Your sight. I repent for everything done knowingly or unknowingly that was against Your Word, Your Will and Your Plan.

I am standing in the gap and asking for Your Forgiveness, Mercy and Grace. Thank You for forgiving us and giving us the grace to not repeat these sins anymore and to not fall into temptation (Matthew 26:41) all the days of our full, long, prosperous, joyful, healthy, safe, and protected lives.

Forgive us, Father, for we do not always know what we do and the consequences in the natural and spiritual realm. Help us, Lord, to overcome these temptations, evil desires and repeated offenses. I ask for Your Forgiveness and thank You for forgiving us.

Father God, I cover myself, my family and our bloodline, our future descendants and all of our families, all that we own, all that we have, all that we are stewards of, and all that we hope to be in the Blood of Jesus.

I declare Isaiah 54:17 over myself, my family, the Body of Christ and leaders across this state, nation and the globe that no weapon formed against us shall prosper, and every tongue which rises against us in judgment we shall condemn.

Father, I break every soulish prayer prayed over our lives. I break every false prophecy spoken and come out of agreement with all the words.

All forms of witchcraft are destroyed in Jesus' name. I receive only Your Perfect Will for each of us.

I speak crop failure to all false prophecies and cover us in the Blood of Jesus.

Lord, I ask that You would stop, intervene and intercept any battle that would be planned against us. That no harm would come near anyone of us.

God, show us all ungodly roots that need to be removed from us and fill them with Your righteousness in Jesus' name. Help us, Lord, to overcome these temptations, evil desires and repeat offenses. We cannot do this in our own strength. We are desperate for You to change us and radically transform us.

Lord I know You do not bless disobedience and it is up to You how much You will extend Your Grace and Mercy. Help us to see Your Truth and be set free in Jesus' name.

Father, according to Galatians 5:22-23, let the fruit of the Spirit rise up in us where we walk with love, joy, peace, forbearance (patience), kindness, goodness, faithfulness, gentleness, and self-control. We also desire to have the gifts according to 1 Corinthians 12. Help us to grow in gifts of wisdom, knowledge, faith, gifts of healing, miraculous powers, prophecy, distinguishing between spirits, speaking in different kinds of tongues, and interpretation of tongues.

We desire to walk in miracles, signs and wonders; knowing You more intimately, hearing Your heartbeat and hearing Your every Word. It is not by our power and might, but only by the Power and Authority of Your Holy Spirit. Thank You, Lord, that You hear the cries of our hearts. Help us to be all that You have created us to be in Jesus' name.

According to Zechariah 4:6, *"Not by might nor by power, but by my Spirit', says the Lord Almighty."*

Prayers of Protection

PSALM 91 -

We dwell in the Secret Place of the Most High and abide under the Shadow of the Almighty. We say that You, Lord, are our refuge and our fortress; Our God, in You we trust. Thank You, Lord, for delivering us from the snare of the fowler and from the perilous pestilence. Thank You for covering us with Your feathers, and under Your wings we take refuge; Your truth is our shield and buckler. We are not afraid of the terror by night, nor the arrow that flies by day, nor the pestilence that walks in darkness, nor of the destruction that lays waste at noonday. Although a thousand may fall at our side, and ten thousand at our right hand; it will not come near us. Only with our eyes will we look, and see the reward of the wicked. Because we have made You, Lord our refuge, the Most High, our dwelling place, no evil shall befall us, nor shall any plague come near our dwelling. You have given Your angels charge over us, to keep us in all Your ways.

In their hands they shall bear us up, lest we dash our foot against a stone. When we tread upon the lion and the cobra, the young lion and the serpent we shall trample underfoot.

Because we have set our love upon You, Lord, You deliver us; You will set us on high, because we have known Your Name. When we call upon You, You will answer us; You are with us in trouble; You deliver us and honor us. With long life You satisfy us, and show us Your Salvation. I pray all this in Jesus name. Amen.

PSALM 23 -

Lord, You are our shepherd; we shall not want. You make us to lie down in green pastures; leading us beside still waters. You restore our soul; You lead us in paths of righteousness for Your name's sake. Yea, though we walk through the valley of the shadow of death, we will fear no evil; For You are with us; Your rod and Your staff, they comfort us. You prepare a table before us in the presence of our enemies; You anoint our head with oil; Our cup runs over. Surely goodness and mercy shall follow us all the days of our life; and we will dwell in the house of the Lord forever. Amen.

Opening Prayer

Father God, we love, honor, and adore You. We bless You, Lord with all that we are and all that we hope to be. We trust in You with all our hearts and lean not on our own understanding. We acknowledge You in all our ways, knowing You will make our path straight (Proverbs 3:5-6).

Thank You, God, for loving us more then we could imagine. Thank You, Lord, for forgiving us exponentially; for giving us strength and grace to not fall into temptation (Matthew 6:13) and to not commit the same sins repeatedly. Lord we repent of our sins and wicked fleshly ways, and we ask for Your Forgiveness. We submit to You, Lord, and resist the devil so that he will flee from us (James 4:7).

Lord, Your Word says if we ask anything in Your name, You will do it (John 14:14). As we pray according to Your Will, Your Written Word, we believe You will answer our prayers (1 John 5:14) in Your perfect timing because You do not lie (Numbers 23:19).

We have full assurance that You hear our prayers (1 John 5:14-15). We come boldly to Your throne of grace in the Mighty Name of Jesus, the name above every name (Hebrews 4:16; Philippians 2:8-11).

✳Lord, I cover myself, my family, all that we own, all for which we have stewardship, and all that we hope to be, in the Blood of Jesus.

I ask that You bless and protect us, our families, our relatives, our friends, all those near and dear to our hearts, the persecuted church, our co-workers, our neighbors, the Body of Christ at our church and across the globe, leaders in this nation and throughout the ends of the Earth. We pray for peace for Israel, America, and the whole Earth.

We thank You, Lord, that we will be all that You created us to be and we will hear "*Well done, good and faithful servant!*" (Matthew 25:23). We thank You that Your Will be done in our lives. Thank You for fine tuning our five senses, for giving us Divine connections and ordering our footsteps; for helping us to be faithful followers of Christ Jesus because of Your Holy Spirit living inside us, Who gives us the grace and supernatural enablement to do all that You called us to do.

Lord, we thank You for blessing us with every spiritual blessing in Christ Jesus (Ephesians 1:3). Thank You for giving us Your Son, who shed His Blood for us while we were still sinners and has redeemed us from our sins (Ephesians 1:7).

Jesus, who knew no sin (2 Corinthians 5:21) came to Earth as a mere man, became sin for us, and paid the ultimate price for us with His life. We thank You, God, from the bottom of our hearts.

Lord, we thank You for spiritual wisdom, discernment, knowledge and understanding and for showing us how to use these gifts according to Your Will, as You have brought unity to all things in heaven and on Earth under Christ.

Thank You for giving us the Mind of Christ and for filling our mouths as we open them. Thank You for giving us favor in high places with God and man (Luke 2:52).

Thank You for prospering us even as our souls prosper (3 John 1:2) and for guidance in dealing with our finances and everything for which we have been made stewards; for opening right doors and closing wrong doors. Thank You for working all things out according to the purpose of Your Will. Thank You, Lord, for salvation, for the truth of Your Word, for helping us believe in You and sealing us with Your Holy Spirit, which is a guarantee of our inheritance from You.

Help us, Lord, to have spiritual discipline to read and study Your Word, pray, fast, declare and decree Your Word and see it established. Break our hearts for the things that break Yours and give us the creativity in taking righteous actions.

Lord, put our faces in front of those You want to pray for us and those for whom You want us to pray for.

Lord, thank You for the Spirit of wisdom and revelation, so that we may know You better. Thank You for saving us and our family members and for making us believers in Jesus Christ who are on fire for You, Lord, walking in all Your ways.

Ephesians Scripture Prayer

Ephesians 1-6 (NKJV)

Lord, thank You for giving us Your Grace and Peace, and for helping us to be faithful followers of Christ Jesus and helping us to finish strong in the Name of Jesus.

Thank You for every Spiritual Blessing we have in heavenly realms because we are united with Christ. Before You ever created the world, You loved us and chose us to be holy without blame in Your eyes. Thank You for bringing us into Your family through the Spirit of Adoption and Sonship through Jesus Christ, Our Savior, which gave You great pleasure. Thank You for Your Glorious Grace that You have poured out on us who belong to Christ Jesus. Thank You for all the Spiritual Gifts You have bestowed upon us. May we walk with Your Grace and Peace all the days of our full, long, healthy, and fruitful lives.

We praise You Lord, our Father of our Lord Jesus Christ, who has blessed us in heavenly realms with every spiritual blessing in Christ. We praise You for choosing us before the creation of the world to be holy and blameless in Your sight. In Love, You have predestined us from adoption to sonship through Jesus Christ, in accordance with Your pleasure and will to the praise of Your Glorious Grace, which You have freely given us. Thank You that in Jesus we have redemption through the Blood of Christ, the forgiveness of sins, in accordance with the riches of Your Grace and Mercy that You lavished on us. With all wisdom and understanding You made known to us the mystery of Your Will according to Your good pleasure, which You purposed in Christ, to be put in effect when times reach their fulfillment to bring unity to all things in heaven and Earth under Christ. Thank You for choosing us and predestining us according to Your plan, working every-thing in conformity with the purpose of Your Will. Thank You that our hope is in Christ and to Him be the Glory.

Thank You that we are included in Christ, as we heard the message of truth, the gospel of our salvation. Thank You, Heavenly Father, for marking us with Your seal, the promised Holy Spirit, guaranteeing our inheritance until the redemption of those who are God's possession to the praise of Your Glory. Lord, may we continue in an attitude of gratitude, to thank You all the days of our long, full, joyful, healthy, prosperous, and safe lives. May our prayers be in accordance to Your Will, Purpose, and Plan, and avail much.

Thank You, Lord, for the eyes of our heart, which are enlightened in order that we may know the hope to which You have called us, the riches of Your glorious inheritance, and Your great power for us who believe. Thank You, Lord, for the power and authority of Your Holy Spirit, who raised Christ from the dead to be seated at Your right hand in heaven.

Thank You for giving us that same power and authority to put ALL things under our feet, to live a victorious life in abundance.

Thank You that we are the head and not the tail, above and not beneath. Thank You that Jesus is the Head over His body, the Church, and that we are the Body of Christ.

Thank You, Lord, that we are made Alive in Christ who strengthens us; that we are dead to sin and alive unto righteousness; that we choose to live righteous and holy lives, which is pleasing in Your sight.

Thank You that we no longer follow the ways of this world but follow You and You alone, no longer gratifying the cravings of our flesh nor following its desires and thoughts. We thank You, Lord, for Your great love for us, for You are rich in mercy and loving kindness.

Lord, our hope is in You. Thank You for the Blood of Jesus which was the only acceptable payment for our sins. According to 1 Peter 1:18-19, Jesus paid the ransom to save us from the empty life we inherited from our ancestors. And the ransom He paid was not mere gold or silver. He paid for us with the precious lifeblood of Christ, the sinless, spotless Lamb of God. By Your Grace and unmerited favor, we have been saved and can enjoy eternity in heaven with You.

Thank You for the precious gift of salvation which was given to us by faith and not by work anyone of us can boast of because it was given to us because of Your Love for us. Lord, our foundation is in You, our Chief Cornerstone, The Rock on which we build all things.

Our foundation is firm and rooted, and grounded in You; built on The Rock we will not fall. We are grateful to You for giving us the gift of revelation as You unfold the mysteries, making them known to us as we seek You above everything else.

42

Lord, Your Spirit strengthens our inner man because Christ dwells in our hearts through faith. Rooted and grounded in Your Love and in Your Word, we have the power to grasp how wide, how long, how high and how deep is Your love. We are aware of Your Fullness in us, Lord, and according to Your Power at work within us to live our lives worthy of the calling we have received, to You be glory forever and ever.

We are grateful that in Christ through faith we may approach You, Father God, with freedom and confidence. Your Son, Jesus, our Lord, has made us free! We are no longer infants, tossed back and forth by the waves, nor are we blown here and there by every wind of teaching or by the cunning and craftiness of people in their deceitful scheming. But instead, we speak the truth in love, and as we grow, we will respect Your mature body whose head is Christ.

We are part of Your whole body, joined and held together by every supporting ligament that grows and builds itself up in love, as each part does its work.

Thank You for the gifts You have given us, those apostles, prophets, evangelists, pastors and teachers, who help equip us for the work of service. With their help, the Body of Christ may be built up until we all reach unity in faith and knowledge of the Son of God and become mature, attaining to the whole measure of the fullness of Christ.

We are Your servants and are hidden in You, our Rock, our Redeemer and our Savior. Lord, thank You for helping us to be completely humble and gentle; to be patient, bearing with one another in love; to make every effort to keep the unity of the Spirit through the bond of peace.

Thank You, Lord, for Your instructions to live sanctified Christian Lives; we no longer indulge in impurity or greed but are generous and loving people. We know the truth and are set free. We are no longer corrupted by deceitful desires. We have a new attitude in our minds and put on the new self, created to be like God in true righteousness and holiness.

We put off falsehood and speak truthfully to our neighbor, for we are all members of one body.

In our anger we do not sin. We do not let the sun go down while we are still angry and therefore do not give the devil a foothold. We do useful things with our hands and share with those in need. We do not let any unwholesome talk come out of our mouths, but only that which is helpful for building others up according to their needs, that it may benefit those who listen. We do not grieve the Holy Spirit of God, with whom we were sealed for the day of redemption.

We rid ourselves of all bitterness, rage and anger, brawling and slander, along with every form of malice. We are kind and compassionate to one another, forgiving each other, just as in Christ, God forgave us.

We follow God's example so we are dearly loved children and walk in the way of love, just as Christ loved us and gave Himself up for us as a fragrant offering and sacrifice to God.

We avoid greed, sexual immorality and any kind of impurity, because we are God's holy people.

We are not deceived with empty words and do not partner with them. We use to be in darkness but now we are in the Light in the Lord and live as children of Light. Fruit of the Light consists of goodness, righteousness and truth, which pleases You. We avoid the fruitless deeds of darkness which is exposed by the Light and is visible.

Everything that is illuminated becomes a Light. The Light of Christ is shining in and through us. We are careful as we live and are wise making the most of every opportunity You give to us.

We are not foolish, but understand Your Will and the plans You have for each of our lives. We do not get drunk on wine, which leads to debauchery (excessive indulgence in sensual pleasures). Rather, we are filled with the Spirit, speaking to one another with psalms, hymns, and songs from the Spirit.

We sing and make music from our hearts to You, Lord, while always giving thanks to You, our Father.

We submit to one another out of reverence for Christ. Wives submit to their husbands as unto the Lord. Husbands are head of their wife as Christ is the head of the church, His body, of which He is the Savior. The church submits to Christ, and so wives submit to their husband in everything.

Husbands love their wives, just as Christ loved the church and gave Himself up for her to make her holy. He cleansed her by washing her with the water through the Word, and presented her to Himself as a radiant church without blemish, but holy and blameless. Husbands, in this same way, love their wives as their own bodies because he who loves his wife loves himself. We care for our own bodies as Christ cares for The Body of Christ, and as we are members of His Body. Husbands love their wives as they love themselves, and wives respect their husbands.

Our children obey and honor their parents in the Lord, for this is right. This is God's first commandment with a promise so that it may go well with you and that you may enjoy long life on the Earth (Ephesians 6:3). Fathers do not exasperate (irritate or infuriate) their children; instead, they bring them up in the training and instruction of the Lord.

We serve wholeheartedly, as if we were serving the Lord, not people, because we know that the Lord will reward each one of us for whatever good we do. We know there is no favoritism with You Lord, and as You do for one, You will do for another because You are no respecter of persons (Acts 10:34). We are strong in You, Lord, and in Your Mighty Power.

We wear the full armor of God continuously, so that we can take our stand against the devil's schemes. We know that our struggle is not against flesh and blood, but against the rulers, against the authorities, against the powers of this dark world and against the spiritual forces of evil in heavenly realms.

We are covered in the full armor of God and wear it continuously even as we sleep. When evil comes, we are able to stand our ground, and after we have done everything, we remain standing. We stand firm with the belt of truth buckled around our waist, with the breastplate of righteousness in place, and with our feet fitted with the readiness that comes from the gospel of peace. We take up the shield of faith and can extinguish all the flaming arrows of the evil one. We take the helmet of salvation and the sword of the Spirit, which is the Word of God.

We pray in the Spirit on all occasions and with every kind of prayer, for all of our requests. We are alert and always keep praying for all of God's people. We pray for our leaders, especially church and government leaders.

We pray, declare, and seal this in the Mighty and Precious Name of Jesus. Amen.

The Whole Armor of God

Helmet of Salvation – Protects our mind when Satan tries to bombard us with lies, ungodly thoughts, doubt, unbelief, and everything that opposes the Word of God.

Breast Plate of Righteousness – Protects our heart when Satan tries to attack our emotions with his lies and everything that opposes the Word of God. Satan even tries to use people to hurt us.

Sword of the Spirit – The Word of God protects us from the lies of Satan. When we speak the Word of God the darkness flees and the Light radiates the Truth. Strength, clarity and all we need will rise up in us.

Belt of Truth – Protects our will. Helps us to fight the lies of Satan with the Word of God.

Shield of Faith – Protects us from Satan when he tries to tempt us or when he tries to cause us to be stagnant and backslide. It protects us from the fiery arrows.

Gospel of Peace – Helps us to spread the Good News of the Gospel. Satan tries his best to prevent the Gospel from spreading across the world. He will do whatever he can to silence our voices. Father God desires the whole world to hear and receive the Gospel which will bring the unsaved to salvation and sharing eternity in heaven with Him.

Ephesians Scriptures (NKJV)

THE EPISTLE OF PAUL THE APOSTLE TO THE EPHESIANS

Greeting

1 Paul, an apostle of Jesus Christ by the will of God, `2 Cor 1:1`

To the saints who are in Ephesus, and faithful in Christ Jesus: `Col 1:2`

²Grace to you and peace from God our Father and the Lord Jesus Christ.

Redemption in Christ

³Blessed be the God and Father of our Lord Jesus Christ, who has blessed us with every spiritual blessing in the heavenly places in Christ, ⁴just as He

¹²that we who first trusted in Christ should be to the praise of His glory. ¹³In Him you also *trusted*, after you heard the word of truth, the gospel of your salvation; in whom also, having believed, you were sealed with the Holy Spirit of promise, ¹⁴whoᵃ is the guarantee of our inheritance until the redemption of the purchased possession, to the praise of His glory.

Prayer for Spiritual Wisdom

¹⁵Therefore I also, after I heard of your faith in the Lord Jesus and your love for all the saints, ¹⁶do not

Greeting

Ephesians 1:2 "¹Paul, an apostle of Jesus Christ by the will of God, To the saints who are in Ephesus, and faithful in Christ Jesus: ²Grace to you and peace from God our Father and the Lord Jesus Christ."

Redemption in Christ

Ephesians 1:3-14 "³Blessed *be* the God and Father of our Lord Jesus Christ, who has blessed us with every spiritual blessing in the heavenly *places* in Christ, ⁴just as He chose us in Him before the foundation of the world, that we should be holy and without blame before Him in love, ⁵having pre-destined us to adoption as sons by Jesus Christ to Himself, according to the good pleasure of His will, ⁶to the praise of the glory of His grace, by which He made us accepted in the Beloved. ⁷In Him we have redemption through His blood, the forgiveness of sins, according to the riches of His grace ⁸which He made to abound toward us in all wisdom and prudence, ⁹having made known to us the mystery of His will, according to His good pleasure which He purposed in Himself, ¹⁰that in the dispensation of the fullness of the times He might gather together in one all things in Christ, both which are in heaven and which are on earth—in Him. ¹¹In Him also we have obtained an inheritance, being predestined according to the purpose of Him who works all things according to the counsel of His will,

[12]that we who first trusted in Christ should be to the praise of His glory. [13]In Him you also *trusted*, after you heard the word of truth, the gospel of your salvation; in whom also, having believed, you were sealed with the Holy Spirit of promise, [14]who is the guarantee of our inheritance until the redemption of the purchased possession, to the praise of His glory."

Prayer for Spiritual Wisdom

Ephesians 1:15-23 "[15] Therefore I also, after I heard of your faith in the Lord Jesus and your love for all the saints, [16] do not cease to give thanks for you, making mention of you in my prayers: [17] that the God of our Lord Jesus Christ, the Father of glory, may give to you the spirit of wisdom and revelation in the knowledge of Him, [18] the eyes of your understanding being enlightened; that you may know what is the hope of His calling, what are the riches of the glory of His inheritance in the saints, [19] and what is the exceeding greatness of His power toward us who believe, according to the working of His mighty power [20] which He worked in Christ when He raised Him from the dead and seated Him at His right hand in the heavenly places, [21] far above all principality and power and might and dominion, and every name that is named, not only in this age but also in that which is to come. [22] And He put all things under His feet, and gave Him to be head over all things to the church,[23] which is His body, the fullness of Him who fills all in all."

By Grace Through Faith

Ephesians 2:1-10 "[1]And you *He made alive,* who were dead in trespasses and sins, [2] in which you once walked according to the course of this world, according to the prince of the power of the air, the spirit who now works in the sons of disobedience, [3] among whom also we all once conducted ourselves in the lusts of our flesh, fulfilling the desires of the flesh and of the mind, and were by nature children of wrath, just as the others. [4] But God, who is rich in mercy, because of His great love with which He loved us, [5] even when we were dead in trespasses, made us alive together with Christ (by grace you have been saved), [6] and raised *us* up together, and made *us* sit together in the heavenly *places* in Christ Jesus, [7] that in the ages to come He might show the exceeding riches of His grace in *His* kindness toward us in Christ Jesus. [8] For by grace you have been saved through faith, and that not of yourselves; it is the gift of God, [9] not of works, lest anyone should boast. [10] For we are His workmanship, created in Christ Jesus for good works, which God prepared beforehand that we should walk in them."

Brought Near by His Blood

Ephesians 2:11-13 "[11] Therefore remember that you, once Gentiles in the flesh—who are called Uncircumcision by what is called the Circumcision made in the flesh by hands—[12] that at that time you were without Christ, being aliens from the commonwealth of Israel and strangers from the covenants of promise, having no hope and without God in the world. [13] But now in Christ Jesus you who once were far off have been brought near by the blood of Christ."

Christ Our Peace

Ephesians 2:14-18 "[14] For He Himself is our peace, who has made both one, and has broken down the middle wall of separation, [15] having abolished in His flesh the enmity, *that is,* the law of commandments *contained* in ordinances, so as to create in Himself one new man *from* the two, *thus* making peace, [16] and that He might reconcile them both to God in one body through the cross, thereby putting to death the enmity. [17] And He came and preached peace to you who were afar off and to those who were near. [18] For through Him we both have access by one Spirit to the Father."

Christ Our Cornerstone

Ephesians 2:19-22 "[19] Now, therefore, you are no longer strangers and foreigners, but fellow citizens with the saints and members of the household of God, [20] having been built on the foundation of the apostles and prophets, Jesus Christ Himself being the chief corner*stone,* [21] in whom the whole building, being fitted together, grows into a holy temple in the Lord, [22] in whom you also are being built together for a dwelling place of God in the Spirit."

The Mystery Revealed

Ephesians 3:1-7 "[1]For this reason I, Paul, the prisoner of Christ Jesus for you Gentiles— [2]if indeed you have heard of the dispensation of the grace of God which was given to me for you, [3]how that by revelation He made known to me the mystery (as I have briefly written already, [4]by which, when you read, you may understand my knowledge in the mystery of Christ), [5]which in other ages was not made known to the sons of men, as it has now been revealed by the Spirit to His holy apostles and prophets: [6]that the Gentiles should be fellow heirs, of the same body, and partakers of His promise in Christ through the gospel, [7]of which I became a minister according to the gift of the grace of God given to me by the effective working of His power."

Purpose of the Mystery

Ephesians 3:8-13 "[8]To me, who am less than the least of all the saints, this grace was given, that I should preach among the Gentiles the unsearchable riches of Christ, [9]and to make all see what *is* the fellowship of the mystery, which from the beginning of the ages has been hidden in God who created all things through Jesus Christ; [10] to the intent that now the manifold wisdom of God might be made known by the church to the principalities and powers in the heavenly *places,* [11] according to the eternal purpose which He accomplished in Christ Jesus our Lord, [12] in whom we have boldness and access with confidence through faith in Him. [13] Therefore I ask that you do not lose heart at my tribulations for you, which is your glory."

Appreciation of the Mystery

Ephesians 3:14-21 "[14] For this reason I bow my knees to the Father of our Lord Jesus Christ, [15] from whom the whole family in heaven and earth is named, [16] that He would grant you, according to the riches of His glory, to be strengthened with might through His Spirit in the inner man, [17] that Christ may dwell in your hearts through faith; that you, being rooted and grounded in love, [18] may be able to comprehend with all the saints what *is* the width and length and depth and height— [19] to know the love of Christ which passes knowledge; that you may be filled with all the fullness of God. [20] Now to Him who is able to do exceedingly abundantly above all that we ask or think, according to the power that works in us, [21] to Him *be* glory in the church by Christ Jesus to all generations, forever and ever. Amen."

Walk in Unity

Ephesians 4:1-6 "¹I, therefore, the prisoner of the Lord, beseech you to walk worthy of the calling with which you were called, ²with all lowliness and gentleness, with longsuffering, bearing with one another in love, ³endeavoring to keep the unity of the Spirit in the bond of peace. ⁴*There is* one body and one Spirit, just as you were called in one hope of your calling; ⁵one Lord, one faith, one baptism; ⁶one God and Father of all, who *is* above all, and through all, and in you all."

Spiritual Gifts

Ephesians 4:7-16 "⁷But to each one of us grace was given according to the measure of Christ's gift. ⁸Therefore He says: "When He ascended on high, He led captivity captive, And gave gifts to men." ⁹(Now this, "He ascended"—what does it mean but that He also first descended into the lower parts of the earth? ¹⁰He who descended is also the One who ascended far above all the heavens, that He might fill all things.) ¹¹And He Himself gave some *to be* apostles, some prophets, some evangelists, and some pastors and teachers, ¹²for the equipping of the saints for the work of ministry, for the edifying of the body of Christ, ¹³till we all come to the unity of the faith and of the knowledge of the Son of God, to a perfect man, to the measure of the stature of the fullness of Christ; [14] that we should no longer be children, tossed to and fro and carried about with every wind of doctrine, by the trickery of men, in the cunning craftiness of deceitful plotting, [15] but, speaking the truth in love, may grow up in all things into Him who is the head—Christ— [16] from whom the whole body, joined and knit together by what every joint supplies, according to the effective working by which every part does its share, causes growth of the body for the edifying of itself in love."

The New Man

Ephesians 4:17-24 "[17] This I say, therefore, and testify in the Lord, that you should no longer walk as the rest of the Gentiles walk, in the futility of their mind, [18] having their understanding darkened, being alienated from the life of God, because of the ignorance that is in them, because of the blindness of their heart; [19] who, being past feeling, have given themselves over to lewdness, to work all uncleanness with greediness. [20] But you have not so learned Christ, [21] if indeed you have heard Him and have been taught by Him, as the truth is in Jesus: [22] that you put off, concerning your former conduct, the old man which grows corrupt according to the deceitful lusts, [23] and be renewed in the spirit of your mind, [24] and that you put on the new man which was created according to God, in true righteousness and holiness."

Do Not Grieve the Spirit

Ephesians 4:25-32 "[25] Therefore, putting away lying, "*Let* each one *of you* speak truth with his neighbor," for we are members of one another.[26] "Be angry, and do not sin": do not let the sun go down on your wrath, [27] nor give place to the devil. [28] Let him who stole steal no longer, but rather let him labor, working with *his* hands what is good, that he may have something to give him who has need. [29] Let no corrupt word proceed out of your mouth, but what is good for necessary edification, that it may impart grace to the hearers. [30] And do not grieve the Holy Spirit of God, by whom you were sealed for the day of redemption. [31] Let all bitterness, wrath, anger, clamor, and evil speaking be put away from you, with all malice. [32] And be kind to one another, tenderhearted, forgiving one another, even as God in Christ forgave you."

Walk in Love

Ephesians 5:1-7 "[1] Therefore be imitators of God as dear children. [2] And walk in love, as Christ also has loved us and given Himself for us, an offering and a sacrifice to God for a sweet-smelling aroma. [3] But fornication and all uncleanness or covetousness, let it not even be named among you, as is fitting for saints; [4] neither filthiness, nor foolish talking, nor coarse jesting, which are not fitting, but rather giving of thanks. [5] For this you know, that no fornicator, unclean person, nor covetous man, who is an idolater, has any inheritance in the kingdom of Christ and God. [6] Let no one deceive you with empty words, for because of these things the wrath of God comes upon the sons of disobedience. [7] Therefore do not be partakers with them."

Walk in Light

Ephesians 5:8-14 "[8] For you were once darkness, but now *you are* light in the Lord. Walk as children of light [9] (for the fruit of the Spirit *is* in all goodness, righteousness, and truth), [10] finding out what is acceptable to the Lord. [11] And have no fellowship with the unfruitful works of darkness, but rather expose *them.* [12] For it is shameful even to speak of those things which are done by them in secret. [13] But all things that are exposed are made manifest by the light, for whatever makes manifest is light. [14] Therefore He says: "Awake, you who sleep, Arise from the dead, And Christ will give you light.""

Walk in Wisdom

Ephesians 5:15-21 "[15] See then that you walk circumspectly, not as fools but as wise, [16] redeeming the time, because the days are evil. [17] Therefore do not be unwise, but understand what the will of the Lord *is.* [18] And do not be drunk with wine, in which is dissipation; but be filled with the Spirit, [19] speaking to one another in psalms and hymns and spiritual songs, singing and making melody in your heart to the Lord, [20] giving thanks always for all things to God the Father in the name of our Lord Jesus Christ, [21] submitting to one another in the fear God."

Marriage—Christ and the Church

Ephesians 5:22-33 "[22] Wives, submit to your own husbands, as to the Lord. [23] For the husband is head of the wife, as also Christ is head of the church; and He is the Savior of the body. [24] Therefore, just as the church is subject to Christ, so *let* the wives *be* to their own husbands in everything. [25] Husbands, love your wives, just as Christ also loved the church and gave Himself for her, [26] that He might sanctify and cleanse her with the washing of water by the word,[27] that He might present her to Himself a glorious church, not having spot or wrinkle or any such thing, but that she should be holy and without blemish.[28] So husbands ought to love their own wives as their own bodies; he who loves his wife loves himself.[29] For no one ever hated his own flesh, but nourishes and cherishes it, just as the Lord *does* the church. [30] For we are members of His body, of His flesh and of His bones. [31] "For this reason a man shall leave his father and mother and be joined to his wife, and the two shall become one flesh." [32] This is a great mystery, but I speak concerning Christ and the church. [33] Nevertheless let each one of you in particular so love his own wife as himself, and let the wife see that she respects her husband."

Children and Parents

Ephesians 6:1-4 "¹Children, obey your parents in the Lord, for this is right. ²"Honor your father and mother," which is the first commandment with promise: ³"that it may be well with you and you may live long on the earth." ⁴And you, fathers, do not provoke your children to wrath, but bring them up in the training and admonition of the Lord."

Bondservants and Masters

Ephesians 6:5-9 "⁵Bondservants, be obedient to those who are your masters according to the flesh, with fear and trembling, in sincerity of heart, as to Christ; ⁶not with eyeservice, as men-pleasers, but as bondservants of Christ, doing the will of God from the heart, ⁷with goodwill doing service, as to the Lord, and not to men, ⁸knowing that whatever good anyone does, he will receive the same from the Lord, whether *he is* a slave or free. ⁹And you, masters, do the same things to them, giving up threatening, knowing that your own Master also is in heaven, and there is no partiality with Him."

The Whole Armor of God

Ephesians 6:10-20 "¹⁰Finally, my brethren, be strong in the Lord and in the power of His might. ¹¹ Put on the whole armor of God, that you may be able to stand against the wiles of the devil.¹² For we do not wrestle against flesh and blood, but against principalities, against powers, against the rulers of the darkness of this age, against spiritual *hosts* of wickedness in the heavenly *places.* ¹³ Therefore take up the whole armor of God, that you may be able to withstand in the evil day, and having done all, to stand. ¹⁴ Stand therefore, having girded your waist with truth, having put on the breastplate of righteousness, ¹⁵ and having shod your feet with the preparation of the gospel of peace; ¹⁶ above all, taking the shield of faith with which you will be able to quench all the fiery darts of the wicked one. ¹⁷ And take the helmet of salvation, and the sword of the Spirit, which is the word of God; ¹⁸ praying always with all prayer and supplication in the Spirit, being watchful to this end with all perseverance and supplication for all the saints— ¹⁹ and for me, that utterance may be given to me, that I may open my mouth boldly to make known the mystery of the gospel, ²⁰ for which I am an ambassador in chains; that in it I may speak boldly, as I ought to speak."

A Gracious Greeting

Ephesians 6:21-24 "²¹ But that you also may know my affairs *and* how I am doing, Tychicus, a beloved brother and faithful minister in the Lord, will make all things known to you; ²² whom I have sent to you for this very purpose, that you may know our affairs, and *that* he may comfort your hearts. [23] Peace to the brethren, and love with faith, from God the Father and the Lord Jesus Christ. [24] Grace *be* with all those who love our Lord Jesus Christ in sincerity. Amen."

Colossians Scripture Prayer

Colossians 1-4 (NKJV)

Lord, thank You for giving us Your Grace and Peace, for helping us to be faithful followers of Christ Jesus and helping us to finish strong. Father help us to pray always and when we know not what to pray, we will pray in the Spirit. Help our love for the saints to continue to grow.

Thank You for the treasures You have laid up for us in heaven, for the Truth of Your Word that bears much fruit. Thank You for helping us to decree a thing and see it established, calling those things that are not as though they are.

We are grateful to You for filling us with Your Knowledge, Wisdom, Discernment and Understanding. Help us to walk worthy of You Lord and be fully pleasing to You in our mind, will and emotions. That we be fruitful in every good work and are increasing in the knowledge of You Lord.

Thank You for strengthening us with all might, according to Your Glorious power, for all patience and longsuffering with joy; giving thanks to You, Father who has qualified us to be partakers of the inheritance of the saints in the light. You have delivered us from the power of darkness and conveyed us into the kingdom of Your Son whom You love, in whom we have redemption through His blood, the forgiveness of sins.

Jesus is the image of the invisible God, the firstborn over all creation. For by Him all things were created that are in heaven and that are on Earth, visible and invisible, whether thrones or dominions or principalities or powers.

All things were created through Him and for Him. And He is before all things, and in Him all things consist. Thank You, Lord, for making Him the head of the body, the church, which we will follow and obey.

Thank You, Father God, for reconciling all things to You. Thank You for the Blood of Jesus that sanctifies and protects. Thank You for reconciling us to be holy, and blameless, and above reproach in Your sight. Help us to continue to move on the straight and narrow path that You predestined us before the foundation of the world.

Help us to be good stewards of all you have given, are giving, and will give to us. Continue to reveal the plans You have for each of our lives and to help us walk in them. Jesus is our hope of Glory.

Thank You, Lord, for continuing to encourage and build us up each day, knitting us together in love for the same goal and purpose to see Christ Glorified through our lives.

Thank You for keeping us rooted and grounded in You and Your Word to be strengthened in our inner man ever increasing in faith. Help us to continue to have an attitude of gratitude, praise and thanksgiving. Help us not to believe any lies nor walk in the flesh but instead know the truth and walk in the Spirit. Help us to be complete in You who is the head of all principality and power.

We thank You that Jesus disarmed principalities and powers, making them a public spectacle, triumphing over them in it. We have been raised with Christ, and will continue to seek those things which are above, where Christ is, sitting at the right hand of God. Setting our minds on things above, not on things on the Earth. For our life is hidden with Christ.

Thank You for helping us to be successful in not falling into traps of sin such as anger, wrath, malice, blasphemy, filthy language coming out of our mouths. That we not lie to one another because we are new creations in Christ. Instead, we are loving and tender-hearted, kind, meek, patient, bearing with one another, forgiving one another.

We walk in the Love of God. Your Perfect Love, Lord, casts out all fear and Your Love is shed aboard in our hearts by the Holy Spirit. We have the peace of God and let it rule our hearts. We let the Word of Christ dwell in us richly in all wisdom, teaching and admonishing one another in psalms and hymns and spiritual songs, singing with grace in our hearts to You, Lord. Whatever we do in word or deed, we do all in the name of the Lord Jesus, giving thanks to You Father.

A wife submits to her own husband, as is fitting in the Lord and a husband, loves his wife and is not bitter toward her. Children, obey their parents in all things, for this is well pleasing to the Lord.

Fathers, do not provoke your children, so they will not become discouraged.

We are all bondservants to You Lord, obeying You in all things. We are not men-pleasers, but have sincerity of heart, fearing You Lord with a reverent fear. All that we do is heartily onto You Lord and not to men, knowing that we will receive the reward of the inheritance from You, Lord, be-cause we are serving the Lord Christ representing Him properly in all things. We do not pay wrong for wrong nor hold grudges.

We continue earnestly in prayer, being vigilant in it with thanksgiving; meanwhile praying also for all mankind.

Father God open doors for us that no man can open and shut doors for us that no man can shut. We walk in wisdom and Godly counsel. We thank You, Lord, for redeeming our time. Helping our speech always to be with grace, seasoned with salt, that we may know how we ought to answer each one. Help our prayers to be fervent that we are able to stand perfect and complete in Your Will.

Colossians Scriptures (NKJV)

COLOSSIANS

Greeting

1 Paul, an apostle of Jesus Christ by the will of God, and Timothy our brother,   Eph. 1:1

[2] To the saints and faithful brethren in Christ *who are* in Colosse: 1 Cor. 4:17

Grace to you and peace from God our Father and the Lord Jesus Christ.[a]

Their Faith in Christ

[3] give thanks to the God and Father

with all might, according to His g[...] ous power, for all patience and [...] suffering with joy; [12]giving th[...] to the Father who has qualified [...] be partakers of the inheritance o[...] saints in the light. [13]He has deliv[...] us from the power of darkness [...] conveyed *us* into the kingdom o[...] Son of His love, [14]in whom we hav[...] demption through His blood,[a] th[...] giveness of sins.

[15]He is the image of the invisib[...] the firstborn over all crea[...]

73

Greeting

Colossians 1:1-2 "[1]Paul, an apostle of Jesus Christ by the will of God, and Timothy our brother, [2] To the saints and faithful brethren in Christ who are in Colosse: Grace to you and peace from God our Father and the Lord Jesus Christ."

Their Faith in Christ

Colossians 1:3-8 "[3]We give thanks to the God and Father of our Lord Jesus Christ, praying always for you, [4]since we heard of your faith in Christ Jesus and of your love for all the saints; [5] because of the hope which is laid up for you in heaven, of which you heard before in the word of the truth of the gospel, [6]which has come to you, as it has also in all the world, and is bringing forth fruit, as it is also among you since the day you heard and knew the grace of God in truth; [7]as you also learned from Epaphras, our dear fellow servant, who is a faithful minister of Christ on your behalf, [8]who also declared to us your love in the Spirit."

Preeminence of Christ

Colossians 1:9-18 "[9]For this reason we also, since the day we heard it, do not cease to pray for you, and to ask that you may be filled with the knowledge of His will in all wisdom and spiritual understanding; [10] that you may walk worthy of the Lord, fully pleasing *Him,* being fruitful in every good work and increasing in the knowledge of God; [11] strengthened with all might, according to His glorious power, for all patience and longsuffering with joy; [12] giving thanks to the Father who has qualified us to be partakers of the inheritance of the saints in the light. [13] He has delivered us from the power of darkness and conveyed *us* into the kingdom of the Son of His love, [14] in whom we have redemption through His blood, the forgiveness of sins. [15] He is the image of the invisible God, the firstborn over all creation. [16] For by Him all things were created that are in heaven and that are on earth, visible and invisible, whether thrones or dominions or principalities or powers. All things were created through Him and for Him. [17] And He is before all things, and in Him all things consist. [18] And He is the head of the body, the church, who is the beginning, the firstborn from the dead, that in all things He may have the preeminence."

Reconciled in Christ

Colossians 1:19-23 "[19] For it pleased *the Father that* in Him all the fullness should dwell, [20] and by Him to reconcile all things to Himself, by Him, whether things on earth or things in heaven, having made peace through the blood of His cross. [21] And you, who once were alienated and enemies in your mind by wicked works, yet now He has reconciled [22] in the body of His flesh through death, to present you holy, and blameless, and above reproach in His sight— [23] if indeed you continue in the faith, grounded and steadfast, and are not moved away from the hope of the gospel which you heard, which was preached to every creature under heaven, of which I, Paul, became a minister."

Sacrificial Service for Christ

Colossians 1:24-29 "[24] I now rejoice in my sufferings for you, and fill up in my flesh what is lacking in the afflictions of Christ, for the sake of His body, which is the church, [25] of which I became a minister according to the stewardship from God which was given to me for you, to fulfill the word of God, [26] the mystery which has been hidden from ages and from generations, but now has been revealed to His saints. [27] To them God willed to make known what are the riches of the glory of this mystery among the Gentiles: which is Christ in you, the hope of glory. [28] Him we preach, warning every man and teaching every man in all wisdom, that we may present every man perfect in Christ Jesus. [29] To this *end* I also labor, striving according to His working which works in me mightily."

Not Philosophy but Christ

Colossians 2:1-10 "[1]For I want you to know what a great conflict I have for you and those in Laodicea, and *for* as many as have not seen my face in the flesh, [2] that their hearts may be encouraged, being knit together in love, and *attaining* to all riches of the full assurance of understanding, to the knowledge of the mystery of God, both of the Father and of Christ, [3] in whom are hidden all the treasures of wisdom and knowledge. [4] Now this I say lest anyone should deceive you with persuasive words. [5] For though I am absent in the flesh, yet I am with you in spirit, rejoicing to see your *good* order and the steadfastness of your faith in Christ. [6] As you therefore have received Christ Jesus the Lord, so walk in Him, [7] rooted and built up in Him and established in the faith, as you have been taught, abounding in it with thanksgiving. [8] Beware lest anyone cheat you through philosophy and empty deceit, according to the tradition of men, according to the basic principles of the world, and not according to Christ. [9] For in Him dwells all the fullness of the Godhead bodily; [10] and you are complete in Him, who is the head of all principality and power."

Not Legalism but Christ

Colossians 2:11-23 "[11] In Him you were also circumcised with the circumcision made without hands, by putting off the body of the sins of the flesh, by the circumcision of Christ, [12] buried with Him in baptism, in which you also were raised with *Him* through faith in the working of God, who raised Him from the dead. [13] And you, being dead in your trespasses and the uncircumcision of your flesh, He has made alive together with Him, having forgiven you all trespasses, [14] having wiped out the handwriting of requirements that was against us, which was contrary to us. And He has taken it out of the way, having nailed it to the cross. [15] Having disarmed principalities and powers, He made a public spectacle of them, triumphing over them in it. [16] So let no one judge you in food or in drink, or regarding a festival or a new moon or sabbaths, [17] which are a shadow of things to come, but the substance is of Christ. [18] Let no one cheat you of your reward, taking delight in *false* humility and worship of angels, intruding into those things which he has not seen, vainly puffed up by his fleshly mind, [19] and not holding fast to the Head, from whom all the body, nourished and knit together by joints and ligaments, grows with the increase *that is* from God. [20] Therefore, if you died with Christ from the basic principles of the world, why, as *though* living in the world, do you subject yourselves to regulations— [21] "Do not touch, do not taste, do not handle," [22] which all concern things which perish with the using—according to the commandments and doctrines of men? [23] These things indeed have an appearance of wisdom in self-imposed religion, *false* humility, and neglect of the body, *but are* of no value against the indulgence of the flesh."

Not Carnality but Christ

Colossians 3:1-11 "[1] If then you were raised with Christ, seek those things which are above, where Christ is, sitting at the right hand of God. ² Set your mind on things above, not on things on the earth. ³ For you died, and your life is hidden with Christ in God. ⁴ When Christ who is our life appears, then you also will appear with Him in glory. ⁵ Therefore put to death your members which are on the earth: fornication, uncleanness, passion, evil desire, and covetousness, which is idolatry. ⁶ Because of these things the wrath of God is coming upon the sons of disobedience, ⁷ in which you yourselves once walked when you lived in them. ⁸ But now you yourselves are to put off all these: anger, wrath, malice, blasphemy, filthy language out of your mouth. ⁹ Do not lie to one another, since you have put off the old man with his deeds, ¹⁰ and have put on the new man who is renewed in knowledge according to the image of Him who created him, ¹¹ where there is neither Greek nor Jew, circumcised nor un-circumcised, barbarian, Scythian, slave nor free, but Christ is all and in all."

Character of the New Man

Colossians 3:12-17 "¹² Therefore, as the elect of God, holy and beloved, put on tender mercies, kindness, humility, meekness, longsuffering; ¹³ bearing with one another, and forgiving one another, if anyone has a complaint against another; even as Christ forgave you, so you also must do. ¹⁴ But above all these things put on love, which is the bond of perfection. ¹⁵ And let the peace of God rule in your hearts, to which also you were called in one body; and be thankful.

[16] Let the word of Christ dwell in you richly in all wisdom, teaching and admonishing one another in psalms and hymns and spiritual songs, singing with grace in your hearts to the Lord. [17] And whatever you do in word or deed, do all in the name of the Lord Jesus, giving thanks to God the Father through Him."

The Christian Home

Colossians 3:18-25 "[18] Wives, submit to your own husbands, as is fitting in the Lord. [19] Husbands, love your wives and do not be bitter toward them. [20] Children, obey your parents in all things, for this is well pleasing to the Lord. [21] Fathers, do not provoke your children, lest they become discouraged. [22] Bondservants, obey in all things your masters according to the flesh, not with eyeservice, as men-pleasers, but in sincerity of heart, fearing God. [23] And whatever you do, do it heartily, as to the Lord and not to men, [24] knowing that from the Lord you will receive the reward of the inheritance; for you serve the Lord Christ. [25] But he who does wrong will be repaid for what he has done, and there is no partiality."

Christian Graces; Final Greetings

Colossians 4:1 "[1] Masters, give your bond-servants what is just and fair, knowing that you also have a Master in heaven.

Christian Graces

Colossians 4:2-6 "[2] Continue earnestly in prayer, being vigilant in it with thanksgiving; [3] meanwhile praying also for us, that God would open to us a door for the word, to speak the mystery of Christ, for which I am also in chains, [4] that I may make it manifest, as I ought to speak. [5] Walk in wisdom toward those *who are* outside, redeeming the time. [6] Let your speech always *be* with grace, seasoned with salt, that you may know how you ought to answer each one."

Final Greetings

Colossians 4:7-15 "[7] Tychicus, a beloved brother, faithful minister, and fellow servant in the Lord, will tell you all the news about me. [8] I am sending him to you for this very purpose, that he may know your circumstances and comfort your hearts, [9] with Onesimus, a faithful and beloved brother, who is *one* of you. They will make known to you all things which *are happening* here. [10] Aristarchus my fellow prisoner greets you, with Mark the cousin of Barnabas (about whom you received instructions: if he comes to you, welcome him), [11] and Jesus who is called Justus. These *are my* only fellow workers for the kingdom of God who are of the circumcision; they have proved to be a comfort to me. [12] Epaphras, who is *one* of you, a bondservant of

Christ, greets you, always laboring fervently for you in prayers, that you may stand perfect and complete in all the will of God. [13] For I bear him witness that he has a great zeal for you, and those who are in Laodicea, and those in Hierapolis. [14] Luke the beloved physician and Demas greet you. [15] Greet the brethren who are in Laodicea, and Nymphas and the church that *is* in his house."

Closing Exhortations and Blessing

Colossians 4:16-18 "[16] Now when this epistle is read among you, see that it is read also in the church of the Laodiceans, and that you likewise read the *epistle* from Laodicea. [17] And say to Archippus, "Take heed to the ministry which you have received in the Lord, that you may fulfill it." [18] This salutation by my own hand—Paul. Remember my chains. Grace *be* with you. Amen."

Philemon
Scripture
Prayer

Philemon 1 (NKJV)

Lord, thank You for helping us labor for You and walk in Your Grace, Peace, and Love. Thank You that Jesus continuously intercedes for us, praying for us without ceasing.

Thank You for great joy. The Joy of the Lord is our strength. That we have joy unspeakable. That we experience fullness of joy as we pray and worship You, Lord. Help us to be bold in Christ. Help us Lord to be confident of this very thing, that He who began a good work in us will bring it to completion until the coming of Christ.

Philemon Scriptures (NKJV)

THE EPISTLE OF PAUL THE APOSTLE TO
PHILEMON

Greeting

Paul, a prisoner of Christ Jesus, and Timothy *our* brother,   ver. 9; Eph. 3: 1; 4: 1

To Philemon our beloved *friend* and fellow laborer, [2]to the beloved[a] Apphia, Archippus our fellow soldier, and to the church in your house:

[3]Grace to you and peace from God our Father and the Lord Jesus Christ.

Philemon's Love and Faith

me, that on your behalf he might minister to me in my chains for the gospel. [14]But without your consent I wanted to do nothing, that your good deed might not be by compulsion, as it were, but voluntary.   1 Cor. 16: 17; Phil. 2: 30

[15]For perhaps he departed for a while for this *purpose,* that you might receive him forever, [16]no longer as a slave but more than a slave—a beloved brother, especially to me but how much more to you, both in the flesh and in the Lord.   So Gen. 45: 5, 8

Greeting

Philemon 1:1-3 "¹ Paul, a prisoner of Christ Jesus, and Timothy *our* brother, To Philemon our beloved *friend* and fellow laborer, ² to the beloved Apphia, Archippus our fellow soldier, and to the church in your house: ³ Grace to you and peace from God our Father and the Lord Jesus Christ."

Philemon's Love and Faith

Philemon 1:4-7 "⁴ I thank my God, making mention of you always in my prayers, ⁵ hearing of your love and faith which you have toward the Lord Jesus and toward all the saints, ⁶ that the sharing of your faith may become effective by the acknowledgment of every good thing which is in you in Christ Jesus. ⁷ For we have great joy and consolation in your love, because the hearts of the saints have been refreshed by you, brother."

The Plea for Onesimus

Philemon 1:8-16 "⁸ Therefore, though I might be very bold in Christ to command you what is fitting, ⁹ *yet* for love's sake I rather appeal *to you*— being such a one as Paul, the aged, and now also a prisoner of Jesus Christ— ¹⁰ I appeal to you for my son Onesimus, whom I have begotten *while* in my chains, ¹¹ who once was unprofitable to you, but now is profitable to you and to me. ¹² I am sending him back. You therefore receive him, that is, my own heart, ¹³ whom I wished to keep with me, that on your behalf he might minister to me in my chains for the gospel. ¹⁴ But without your consent I wanted to do nothing, that your good deed might not be by compulsion, as it were, but voluntary. ¹⁵ For perhaps he departed for a while for this *purpose,* that you might receive him forever, ¹⁶ no longer as a slave but more than a slave—a beloved brother, especially to me but how much more to you, both in the flesh and in the Lord."

Philemon's Obedience Encouraged

Philemon 1:17-22 "¹⁷ If then you count me as a partner, receive him as *you would* me. ¹⁸ But if he has wronged you or owes anything, put that on my account. ¹⁹ I, Paul, am writing with my own hand. I will repay—not to mention to you that you owe me even your own self besides. ²⁰ Yes, brother, let me have joy from you in the Lord; refresh my heart in the Lord. ²¹ Having confidence in your obedience, I write to you, knowing that you will do even more than I say. ²² But, meanwhile, also prepare a guest room for me, for I trust that through your prayers I shall be granted to you."

Farewell

Philemon 1:23-25 "[23] Epaphras, my fellow prisoner in Christ Jesus, greets you, [24] *as do* Mark, Aristarchus, Demas, Luke, my fellow laborers. [25] The grace of our Lord Jesus Christ *be* with your spirit. Amen."

Philippians Scripture Prayer

Philippians 1-4 (NKJV)

Thank You, Lord, that we are bondservants of Jesus Christ and walk in Your Grace, Peace and Love. Thank You, Lord, for praying for us without ceasing. For giving us joy unspeakable and fullness of joy. We are confident of this very thing, that He who has begun a good work in us will complete it until the day of Jesus Christ.

Thank You, Lord, that our love abounds more and more in knowledge and all discernment, that we may approve the things that are excellent and be sincere and without offense till the day of Christ, being filled with the fruits of righteousness which are by Jesus Christ, to the glory and praise of God.

Help us to further the gospel, so that it is preached across the globe. Give us greater boldness and confidence to preach Your Word. Help us to be free from selfish ambition and to walk in love. Let our conduct be worthy of the gospel of Christ. Help us to stand fast in one spirit, with one mind striving together for the faith of the gospel, and not in any way be terrified by our adversaries.

Help us to have love, being of one accord, of one mind. Let nothing be done through selfish ambition or conceit, but in lowliness of mind esteeming others better than ourselves. Let each of us look out not only for his own interests, but also for the interests of others. Help us to be humble and obedient to you even to the point of death.

Thank You for Jesus, the name that is above every name. That at the name of Jesus every knee shall bow, of those in heaven, and of those on Earth, and of those under the Earth, and that every tongue should confess that Jesus Christ is Lord, to the glory of God the Father.

Help us Lord to walk out our own salvation with fear and trembling; for it is God who works in us both to will and to do for His good pleasure. Help us not to complain but that we be blameless and harmless, children of God without fault in the midst of a crooked and perverse generation, among whom we shine as lights in the world, holding fast the word of life, so that we may rejoice in the day of Christ that we have not run in vain or labored in vain. We trust in You, Lord, with all our hearts and lean not on our own understanding but acknowledge You, Lord, in all things knowing You will make our paths straight. Thank You that we have Godly character. We rejoice in You, Lord.

We forget those things which are behind and reach forward to those things which are ahead. We press toward the goal for the prize of the upward call of God in Christ Jesus. We are mature in the Lord and have the mind of Christ.

We are examples of Jesus knowing our citizenship is in heaven, from which we also eagerly wait for the Savior, the Lord Jesus Christ. Thank You, Lord, that we finish strong and that our names are in the Book of Life. We rejoice in the Lord always.

We are not anxious for anything, but in everything by prayer and supplication, with thanksgiving, let our requests be made known to

You, Lord, and the peace of God, which surpasses all understanding, will guard your hearts and minds through Christ Jesus.

We meditate on whatever things that are true, whatever things are noble, whatever things are just, whatever things are pure, whatever things are lovely, whatever things are of good report, if there is any virtue and if there is anything praiseworthy.

We prosper and flourish not lacking any beneficial thing. We speak the blessings and promises of God. We have the mind of Christ and can do all things through Christ who strengthens us.

Philippians Scriptures (NKJV)

PHILIPPIANS

Greeting

1 Paul and Timothy, bondservants of Jesus Christ,

To all the saints in Christ Jesus who are in Philippi, with the bishops[a] and deacons: 1 Cor. 1:2

[2]Grace to you and peace from God our Father and the Lord Jesus Christ.

Thankfulness and Prayer

[3]I thank my God upon every remembrance of you, [4]always in every prayer of mine making request for you all with joy, [5]for your fellowship in the

actually turned out for the furtherance of the gospel, [13]so that it has become evident to the whole palace guard, and to all the rest, that my chains are in Christ; [14]and most of the brethren in the Lord, having become confident by my chains, are much more bold to speak the word without fear.   ch. 4:22

[15]Some indeed preach Christ even from envy and strife, and some also from goodwill: [16]The former[a] preach Christ from selfish ambition, not sincerely, supposing to add affliction to my chains; [17]but the latter out of love, knowing that I am appointed for the defense of the gospel. [18]What then? Only that

93

Greeting

Philippians 1:1-2 "¹Paul and Timothy, bondservants of Jesus Christ, To all the saints in Christ Jesus who are in Philippi, with the bishops and deacons: ²Grace to you and peace from God our Father and the Lord Jesus Christ."

Thankfulness and Prayer

Philippians 1:3-11 "³ I thank my God upon every remembrance of you, ⁴ always in every prayer of mine making request for you all with joy, ⁵ for your fellowship in the gospel from the first day until now, ⁶ being confident of this very thing, that He who has begun a good work in you will complete *it* until the day of Jesus Christ; ⁷ just as it is right for me to think this of you all, because I have you in my heart, inasmuch as both in my chains and in the defense and confirmation of the gospel, you all are partakers with me of grace. ⁸ For God is my witness, how greatly I long for you all with the affection of Jesus Christ. ⁹ And this I pray, that your love may abound still more and more in knowledge and all discernment, ¹⁰ that you may approve the things that are excellent, that you may be sincere and without offense till the day of Christ, ¹¹ being filled with the fruits of righteousness which *are* by Jesus Christ, to the glory and praise of God."

Christ Is Preached

Philippians 1:12-18 "[12] But I want you to know, brethren, that the things *which happened* to me have actually turned out for the furtherance of the gospel, [13] so that it has become evident to the whole palace guard, and to all the rest, that my chains are in Christ; [14] and most of the brethren in the Lord, having become confident by my chains, are much more bold to speak the word without fear. [15] Some indeed preach Christ even from envy and strife, and some also from goodwill: [16] The former preach Christ from selfish ambition, not sincerely, supposing to add affliction to my chains;[17] but the latter out of love, knowing that I am appointed for the defense of the gospel. [18] What then? Only *that* in every way, whether in pretense or in truth, Christ is preached; and in this I rejoice, yes, and will rejoice."

To Live Is Christ

Philippians 1:19-26 "[19] For I know that this will turn out for my deliverance through your prayer and the supply of the Spirit of Jesus Christ, [20] according to my earnest expectation and hope that in nothing I shall be ashamed, but with all boldness, as always, so now also Christ will be magnified in my body, whether by life or by death. [21] For to me, to live *is* Christ, and to die is *gain*. [22] But if *I* live on in the flesh, this *will mean* fruit from *my* labor; yet what I shall choose I cannot tell.

^{23} For I am hard-pressed between the two, having a desire to depart and be with Christ, *which* is far better. ^{24} Nevertheless to remain in the flesh is more needful for you. ^{25} And being confident of this, I know that I shall remain and continue with you all for your progress and joy of faith, ^{26} that your rejoicing for me may be more abundant in Jesus Christ by my coming to you again."

Striving and Suffering for Christ

Philippians 1:27-30 "^{27} Only let your conduct be worthy of the gospel of Christ, so that whether I come and see you or am absent, I may hear of your affairs, that you stand fast in one spirit, with one mind striving together for the faith of the gospel, ^{28} and not in any way terrified by your adversaries, which is to them a proof of perdition, but to you of salvation, and that from God. ^{29} For to you it has been granted on behalf of Christ, not only to believe in Him, but also to suffer for His sake, ^{30} having the same conflict which you saw in me and now hear *is* in me."

Unity Through Humility

Philippians 2:1-4 "^{1} Therefore if there is any consolation in Christ, if any comfort of love, if any fellowship of the Spirit, if any affection and mercy, ^{2} fulfill my joy being like-minded, having the same love, *being* of one accord, of one mind.

[3] Let nothing be done through selfish ambition or conceit, but in lowliness of mind let each esteem others better than himself. [4] Let each of you look out not only for his own interests, but also for the interests of others."

The Humbled and Exalted Christ

Philippians 2:5-11 "[5] Let this mind be in you which was also in Christ Jesus, [6] who, being in the form of God, did not consider it robbery to be equal with God, [7] but made Himself of no reputation, taking the form of a bondservant, *and* coming in the likeness of men. [8] And being found in appearance as a man, He humbled Himself and became obedient to *the point of* death, even the death of the cross. [9] Therefore God also has highly exalted Him and given Him the name which is above every name, [10] that at the name of Jesus every knee should bow, of those in heaven, and of those on earth, and of those under the earth, [11] and *that* every tongue should confess that Jesus Christ *is* Lord, to the glory of God the Father."

Light Bearers

Philippians 2:12-18 "[12] Therefore, my beloved, as you have always obeyed, not as in my presence only, but now much more in my absence, work out your own salvation with fear and trembling; [13] for it is God who works in you both to will and to do for *His* good pleasure. [14] Do all things without complaining and disputing, [15] that you may become blameless and harmless, children of God without fault in the midst of a crooked and perverse generation, among whom you shine as lights in the world, [16] holding fast the word of life, so that I may rejoice in the day of Christ that I have not run in vain or labored in vain. [17] Yes, and if I am being poured out *as a drink offering* on the sacrifice and service of your faith, I am glad and rejoice with you all. [18] For the same reason you also be glad and rejoice with me."

Timothy Commended

Philippians 2:19-24 "[19] But I trust in the Lord Jesus to send Timothy to you shortly, that I also may be encouraged when I know your state.[20] For I have no one like-minded, who will sincerely care for your state. [21] For all seek their own, not the things which are of Christ Jesus. [22] But you know his proven character, that as a son with *his* father he served with me in the gospel. [23] Therefore I hope to send him at once, as soon as I see how it goes with me. [24] But I trust in the Lord that I myself shall also come shortly."

Epaphroditus Praised

Philippians 2:25-30 "[25] Yet I considered it necessary to send to you Epaphroditus, my brother, fellow worker, and fellow soldier, but your messenger and the one who ministered to my need; [26] since he was longing for you all, and was distressed because you had heard that he was sick. [27] For indeed he was sick almost unto death; but God had mercy on him, and not only on him but on me also, lest I should have sorrow upon sorrow. [28] Therefore I sent him the more eagerly, that when you see him again you may rejoice, and I may be less sorrowful. [29] Receive him therefore in the Lord with all gladness, and hold such men in esteem; [30] because for the work of Christ he came close to death, not regarding his life, to supply what was lacking in your service toward me."

All for Christ

Philippians 3:1-11 "[1]Finally, my brethren, rejoice in the Lord. For me to write the same things to you *is* not tedious, but for you *it is* safe.[2] Beware of dogs, beware of evil workers, beware of the mutilation! [3] For we are the circumcision, who worship God in the Spirit, rejoice in Christ Jesus, and have no confidence in the flesh, [4] though I also might have confidence in the flesh. If anyone else thinks he may have confidence in the flesh, I more so: [5] circumcised the eighth day, of the stock of Israel, *of* the tribe of Benjamin, a Hebrew of the Hebrews; concerning the law, a Pharisee; [6] concerning zeal, persecuting the church; concerning the righteousness which is in the law, blameless. [7] But what things were gain to me, these I have counted loss for Christ.

⁸ Yet indeed I also count all things loss for the excellence of the knowledge of Christ Jesus my Lord, for whom I have suffered the loss of all things, and count them as rubbish, that I may gain Christ ⁹ and be found in Him, not having my own righteousness, which is from the law, but that which is through faith in Christ, the righteousness which is from God by faith; ¹⁰ that I may know Him and the power of His resurrection, and the fellowship of His sufferings, being conformed to His death, ¹¹ if, by any means, I may attain to the resurrection from the dead."

Pressing Toward the Goal

Philippians 3:12-16 "¹² Not that I have already attained, or am already perfected; but I press on, that I may lay hold of that for which Christ Jesus has also laid hold of me. ¹³ Brethren, I do not count myself to have apprehended; but one thing *I do,* forgetting those things which are behind and reaching forward to those things which are ahead,¹⁴ I press toward the goal for the prize of the upward call of God in Christ Jesus. ¹⁵ Therefore let us, as many as are mature, have this mind; and if in anything you think otherwise, God will reveal even this to you. ¹⁶ Nevertheless, to *the degree* that we have already attained, let us walk by the same rule, let us be of the same mind."

Our Citizenship in Heaven

Philippians 3:17-21 "[17] Brethren, join in following my example, and note those who so walk, as you have us for a pattern. [18] For many walk, of whom I have told you often, and now tell you even weeping, that they are the enemies of the cross of Christ: [19] whose end is destruction, whose god is their belly, and whose glory is in their shame —who set their mind on earthly things. [20] For our citizenship is in heaven, from which we also eagerly wait for the Savior, the Lord Jesus Christ, [21] who will transform our lowly body that it may be conformed to His glorious body, according to the working by which He is able even to subdue all things to Himself."

Be Anxious for Nothing; Think These Thoughts

Philippians 4:1 "[1]Therefore, my beloved and longed-for brethren, my joy and crown, so stand fast in the Lord, beloved."

Be United, Joyful, and in Prayer

Philippians 4:2-7 "[2] I implore Euodia and I implore Syntyche to be of the same mind in the Lord. [3]And I urge you also, true companion, help these women who labored with me in the gospel, with Clement also, and the rest of my fellow workers, whose names are in the Book of Life.

⁴ Rejoice in the Lord always. Again I will say, rejoice! ⁵ Let your gentleness be known to all men. The Lord is at hand. ⁶ Be anxious for nothing, but in everything by prayer and supplication, with thanks-giving, let your requests be made known to God; ⁷ and the peace of God, which surpasses all understanding, will guard your hearts and minds through Christ Jesus."

Meditate on These Things

Philippians 4:8-9 "⁸Finally, brethren, whatever things are true, whatever things are noble, whatever things are just, whatever things are pure, whatever things are lovely, whatever things are of good report, if there is any virtue and if there is anything praiseworthy—meditate on these things. ⁹ The things which you learned and received and heard and saw in me, these do, and the God of peace will be with you."

Philippian Generosity

Philippians 4:10-20 "¹⁰But I rejoiced in the Lord greatly that now at last your care for me has flourished again; though you surely did care, but you lacked opportunity. ¹¹Not that I speak in regard to need, for I have learned in whatever state I am, to be content: ¹²I know how to be abased, and I know how to abound. Everywhere and in all things I have learned both to be full and to be hungry, both to abound and to suffer need. [13] I can do all things through Christ who strengthens me. [14] Nevertheless you have done well that you shared in my distress. [15] Now you Philippians know also that in the beginning of the gospel, when I departed from Macedonia, no church shared with me concerning giving and receiving but you only. [16] For even in Thessalonica you sent aid once and again for my necessities. [17] Not that I seek the gift, but I seek the fruit that abounds to your account. 18 Indeed I have all and abound. I am full, having received from Epaphroditus the things sent from you, a sweet-smelling aroma, an acceptable sacrifice, well pleasing to God. [19] And my God shall sup-ply all your need according to His riches in glory by Christ Jesus. [20] Now to our God and Father be glory forever and ever. Amen."

Greeting and Blessing

Philippians 4:21:23 "[21] Greet every saint in Christ Jesus. The brethren who are with me greet you. [22] All the saints greet you, but especially those who are of Caesar's household. [23] The grace of our Lord Jesus Christ be with you all. Amen."

About the Author

Valerie Mecca was born and raised in the Roman Catholic faith. She became a Spirit-filled, born again believer in Jesus Christ at the age of 45 after having an encounter with Holy Spirit. Valerie heard the Voice of Almighty God say, "Stop analyzing life and start living."

During that moment, her body was filled with the peace of God that surpasses all understanding, and joy unspeakable. This tangible encounter changed her life forever. Moment by moment, day by day, Valerie experiences The Lord in ways she never imagined.

Since 2008 she has been pursuing The Lord through prayer. Valerie serves as an Intercessor and participates in prayer ministries where the Lord leads her.

Her desire to be transformed and changed by the Glory of God resulted in expanding her education, both personally and professionally. Valerie has obtained an Associate Degree and a Bachelor's Degree in Computer Science from St. John's University, Jamaica, New York, a certificate NJ Supervisory Training Empowering Performance (NJ STEP), a Project Management Certificate and an ITIL Foundation Certificate in IT Service Management.

She is the Club Founder of a Toastmasters club in Trenton, NJ. In a short period of time, Valerie obtained the Distinguished Toastmaster accreditation from Toastmasters International, a well-known public speaking and leadership organization.

She has obtained a certificate from the Institute of Biblical Study, a Bachelor's Diploma from Wagner Leadership, a certificate from LeaderLabs Executive Leadership: 10 Essential Skills, and a Diploma from Rhema Correspondence Bible School.

Valerie desires for all creation to know and have a relationship with The Lord (Father God, Jesus and Holy Spirit) and shares her experiences through her website - valsbetterlife.com, her YouTube channel, social media, and public speaking.

Valerie, her husband Paul, and their two wonderful adult children, Arianna and Paul, are experiencing the blessings and faithfulness of The Lord on a daily basis.

She continues to pray for her needs, intercedes for the needs of her family, the Body of Christ, leaders in the United States of America, leaders across the globe and all mankind.

It is her desire that all mankind would have a deep, intimate relationship with Almighty God, and that each person would grow in prayer and intercession, seeing the Will of God being done on Earth as it is in heaven, all for the Glory of God.

Social Media Resources

Valerie's Water Baptism Video –
www.youtube.com/watch?v=Iqsni7S89tw

An Encounter of the Best Kind video –
www.youtube.com/watch?v=GSAkjwdCY2g

Almighty God Does Exist video –
www.youtube.com/watch?
v=X2pNKvCwZSM

Website - valsbetterlife.com

YouTube channel - PRAYERS AND THE
BIBLE https://youtu.be/ocBj_Td-mLQ

Blog - Blog.ValsBetterLife.com

Contact Information

To book Valerie for a speaking engagement or training, please email Valerie@Valsbetterlife.com

Contact Us at - Valerie@ValsBetterLife.com with your comments.

Please provide a book review on Amazon.

End with Faith Scriptures

Mark 11:24, "*Therefore I tell you, whatever you ask for in prayer, believe that you have received it, and it will be yours.*"

James 5:16 (NKJV), "*Confess your trespasses to one another, and pray for one another, that you may be healed. The effective, fervent prayer of a righteous man avails much.*"

Hebrews 11:6, "*And without faith it is impossible to please God, because anyone who comes to him must believe that he exists and that he rewards those who earnestly seek him.*"

May this book stir up your Spirit man to seek the Lord with your whole heart, to find His plan, and purpose for your life in Jesus Name.

Printed in Great Britain
by Amazon

27273923R00066